Christian Motivation Verses

Daily Motivational verses from the Holy Bible with space for your daily thoughts from the following- AMPC, TLB,MSG,NIV,NASB, ESV, AMP, NLT,NKJV

"For God has bought you with a great price. So use every part of your body to give glory back to God because he owns it." (1 Corinthians 6:20, TLB)

Your Daily Notes-

"God can pour on the blessings in astonishing ways so that you're ready for anything and everything, more than just ready to do what needs to be done." (2 Corinthians 9:8, MSG)

Your Daily Notes-

"...We have no power to face this vast army that is attacking us. We do not know what to do, but our eyes are on you." (2 Chronicles 20:12, NIV)

Your Daily Notes-

"Return to the stronghold, O prisoners who have the hope; this very day I am declaring that I will restore double to you." (Zechariah 9:12, NASB)

Your Daily Notes-

"Thanks be to God, who always leads us in triumph through Christ..." (2 Corinthians 2:14, NASB)

Your Daily Notes-

"...with God all things are possible." (Matthew 19:26, NIV)

Your Daily Notes-

"How we praise God, the Father of our Lord Jesus Christ, who has blessed us with every blessing in heaven because we belong to Christ." (Ephesians 1:3, TLB)

Your Daily Notes-

"...You are worried and upset about many things, but few things are needed — or indeed only one. ..."
(Luke 10:41–42, NIV)
Your Daily Notes-

"That is why, for Christ's sake, I delight in weaknesses, in insults, in hardships, in persecutions, in difficulties. For when I am weak, then I am strong." (2 Corinthians 12:10, NIV)

Your Daily Notes-

"...I came that they may have life and have it abundantly." (John 10:10, ESV)

Your Daily Notes-

"When you go through deep waters and great trouble, I will be with you. When you go through rivers of difficulty, you will not drown!" (Isaiah 43:2, TLB)

Your Daily Notes-

"Come to Me, all you who labor and are heavy-laden and overburdened, and I will cause you to rest. [I will ease and relieve and refresh your souls.]" (Matthew 11:28, AMP)

Your Daily Notes-

"Don't be misled — you cannot mock the justice of God. You will always harvest what you plant."
(Galatians 6:7, NLT)
Your Daily Notes-

"No unbelief or distrust made him waver (doubtingly question) concerning the promise of God, but he grew strong and was empowered by faith as he gave praise and glory to God." (Romans 4:20, AMP)

Your Daily Notes-

"The way of the righteous is like the first gleam of dawn, which shines ever brighter until the full light of day." (Proverbs 4:18, NLT)

Your Daily Notes-

"And after the earthquake, there was a fire, but the Lord was not in the fire. And after the fire, there was the sound of a gentle whisper." (1 Kings 19:12, TLB)

Your Daily Notes-

The Lord is my strength and my song; he has given me victory." (Psalm 118:14, NLT)

Your Daily Notes-

“ For I know the plans I have for you,’ declares the Lord, ‘plans to prosper you and not to harm you, plans to give you hope and a future. ” (Jeremiah 29:11, NIV)

Your Daily Notes-

"Our present troubles are small and won't last very long. Yet they produce for us a glory that vastly outweighs them and will last forever!" (2 Corinthians 4:17, NLT)

Your Daily Notes-

"They did not conquer by their own strength and skill, but by your mighty power and because you smiled upon them and favored them." (Psalm 44:3, TLB)

Your Daily Notes-

"For the vision is yet for an appointed time...though it tarry, wait for it" (Habakkuk 2:3, KJV)

Your Daily Notes-

"I will lift up my eyes to the hills. From where does my help come? My help comes from the Lord, who made heaven and earth." (Psalm 121:1–2, ESV)

Your Daily Notes-

"Therefore, let us offer through Jesus a continual sacrifice of praise to God, proclaiming our allegiance to his name." (Hebrews 13:15, NLT)

Your Daily Notes-

"Bring all the tithes (the whole tenth of your income) into the storehouse, that there may be food in My house, and prove Me now by it, says the Lord of hosts, if I will not open the windows of heaven for you and pour you out a blessing, that there shall not be room enough to receive it." (Malachi 3:10, AMP)

Your Daily Notes-

"Do not neglect your gift..." (1 Timothy 4:14, NIV)

Your Daily Notes-

"Instead of shame and dishonor, you will enjoy a double share of honor. You will possess a double portion of prosperity in your land, and everlasting joy will be yours." (Isiah 61:7 NIV)

Your Daily Notes-

"God can miraculously restore your finances" (Joel 2:25-26 NIV)

Your Daily Notes-

"God can flood your life with divine favor" (Psalm 5:12 NIV)

Your Daily Notes-

"God can heal your spirit, soul, and body" (Psalm 103:3-5 NIV)

Your Daily Notes-

"...Let them say continually, 'The LORD be magnified, Who delights in the prosperity of His servant.' "
(Psalm 35:27, NASB)

Your Daily Notes-

"Let the peace of Christ rule in your hearts, since as members of one body you were called to peace. And be thankful." (Colossians 3:15, NIV)

Your Daily Notes-

"I can do all things through Christ who strengthens me." (Philippians 4:13, NKJV)

Your Daily Notes-

"For God is working in you, giving you the desire and the power to do what pleases him."
(Philippians 2:13, NLT)

Your Daily Notes-

" For I know the plans I have for you,' declares the Lord, 'plans to prosper you and not to harm you, plans to give you hope and a future "
(Jeremiah 29:11, NIV)

Your Daily Notes-

"So then, just as you received Christ Jesus as Lord, continues to live in him, rooted and built up in him, strengthened in the faith as you were taught, and overflowing with thankfulness."
(Colossians 2:6–7, NIV)

Your Daily Notes-

"He heals the brokenhearted and binds up their wounds." (Psalm 147:3, NIV)

Your Daily Notes-

"...If God is for us, who can be against us?" (Romans 8:31, NIV)

Your Daily Notes-

"...'Oh, that you would bless me and enlarge my territory!'..." (1 Chronicles 4:10, NIV)

Your Daily Notes-

“The mind of man plans his way, but the LORD directs his steps.” (Proverbs 16:9, NASB)

Your Daily Notes-

“For to us a Child is born, to us a Son is given; and the government shall be upon His shoulder, and His name shall be called Wonderful Counselor, Mighty God, Everlasting Father [of Eternity], Prince of Peace” (Isaiah 9:6, AMP)

Your Daily Notes-

"The simple believe anything, but the prudent give thought to their steps." (Proverbs 14:15, NIV)

Your Daily Notes-

"In his heart a man plans his course, but the LORD determines his steps" (Proverbs 16:9, NIV)

Your Daily Notes-

“For our light and momentary troubles are achieving for us an eternal glory that far outweighs them all”
(2 Corinthians 4:17, NIV)
Your Daily Notes-

“Yes, my soul, find rest in God; my hope comes from him.”(Psalm 62:5, NIV)

Your Daily Notes-

"...O favored one [endued with grace]! The Lord is with you!..."(Luke 1:28, AMP)

Your Daily Notes-

"Cease striving and know that I am God..."(Psalm 46:10, NASB)

Your Daily Notes-

"For God so loved the world that he gave his one and only Son, that whoever believes in him shall not perish but have eternal life."(John 3:16, NIV)

Your Daily Notes-

"So if the Son sets you free, you will be free indeed."(John 8:36, NIV)

Your Daily Notes-

"Let the Lord be magnified, Who has pleasure in the prosperity of His servant." (Psalm 35:27, NKJV)

Your Daily Notes-

"Now to him who is able to do immeasurably more than all we ask or imagine, according to his power that is at work within us." (Ephesians 3:20, NIV)

Your Daily Notes-

"Love never fails..." (1 Corinthians 13:8, NIV)

Your Daily Notes-

"For the LORD God is a sun and shield; the LORD bestows favor and honor; no good thing does he withhold from those whose walk is blameless." (Psalm 84:11, NIV)

Your Daily Notes-

"I waited patiently for the Lord to help me, and he turned to me and heard my cry. He lifted me out of the pit of despair...He set my feet on solid ground...He has given me a new song to sing"
(Psalm 40:1–3, NLT)
Your Daily Notes-

"God can pour on the blessings in astonishing ways so that you're ready for anything and everything, more than just ready to do what needs to be done." (2 Corinthians 9:8, MSG)

Your Daily Notes-

"He gives strength to the weary and increases the power of the weak." (Isaiah 40:29, NIV)

Your Daily Notes-

"Faith is the confidence that what we hope for will actually happen; it gives us assurance about things we cannot see." (Hebrews 11:1, NLT)

Your Daily Notes-

"As the heavens are higher than the earth, so are my ways higher than your ways and my thoughts than your thoughts" (Isaiah 55:9, NIV)

Your Daily Notes-

"I will listen to what God the Lord says; he promises peace to his people..." (Psalm 85:8, NIV)

Your Daily Notes-

“Praise the LORD, my soul, and forget not all his benefits.” (Psalm 103:2, NIV)

Your Daily Notes-

“I have set before you life and death, the blessing and the curse. So choose life in order that you may live” (Deuteronomy 30:19, NASB)

Your Daily Notes-

"Wisdom is supreme—so get wisdom" (Proverbs 4:7, HCSB)

Your Daily Notes-

"'...I will make you like my signet ring, for I have chosen you,' declares the LORD Almighty."
(Haggai 2:23, NIV)

Your Daily Notes-

“Blessed is the one whose transgressions are forgiven, whose sins are covered.” (Psalm 32:1, NIV)

Your Daily Notes-

“I will go before you and make the crooked places straight...” (Isaiah 45:2, NKJV)

Your Daily Notes-

"'I will restore health to you and heal you of your wounds,' says the LORD." (Jeremiah 30:17, NKJV)

Your Daily Notes-

"My grace is sufficient for you, for My strength is made perfect in weakness..." (2 Corinthians 12:9, NKJV)

Your Daily Notes-

"...Seek me and live." (Amos 5:4, NIV)

Your Daily Notes-

"Even though I walk through the valley of the shadow of death, I will fear no evil, for you are with me..."
(Psalm 23:4, ESV)
Your Daily Notes-

"For I am about to do something new. See, I have already begun! Do you not see it?" (Isaiah 43:19, NLT)

Your Daily Notes-

"Then the LORD said to him, 'What is that in your hand?" (Exodus 4:2, NIV)

Your Daily Notes-

"Ask and keep on asking and it will be given to you; seek and keep on seeking and you will find; knock and keep on knocking and the door will be opened to you." (Matthew 7:7, AMP)

Your Daily Notes-

"I will say of the Lord, 'He is my Refuge and my fortress, my God, in whom I trust [with great confidence, and on whom I rely]!'" (Psalm 91:2, AMP)

Your Daily Notes-

“Whatever is true, whatever is noble, whatever is right, whatever is pure, whatever is lovely, whatever is admirable—if anything is excellent or praiseworthy—think about such things.” (Philippians 4:8, NIV)

Your Daily Notes-

“Then the word of the Lord came to Elijah: ‘Leave here, turn eastward and hide in the Kerith Ravine, east of the Jordan. You will drink from the brook, and I have directed the ravens to supply you with food there.’” (1 Kings 17:2–4, NIV)

Your Daily Notes-

"As the rain and the snow come down from heaven, and do not return to it without watering the earth and making it bud and flourish, so that it yields seed for the sower and bread for the eater, so is my word that goes out from my mouth: It will not return to me empty, but will accomplish what I desire and achieve the purpose for which I sent it." (Isaiah 55:10–11, NIV)

Your Daily Notes-

____

____

____

____

____

"There is therefore now no condemnation to those who are in Christ Jesus, who do not walk according to the flesh, but according to the Spirit." (Romans 8:1, NKJV)

Your Daily Notes-

____

____

____

____

____

"Can any one of you by worrying add a single hour to your life?" (Matthew 6:27, NIV)

Your Daily Notes-

"He raised us up together with Him...that in the ages to come He might [clearly] show the immeasurable and unsurpassed riches of His grace..." (Ephesians 2:6–7, AMP)

Your Daily Notes-

"Do not be conformed to this world, but be transformed by the renewing of your mind..."
(Romans 12:2, NASB)
Your Daily Notes-

"...I came that they may have and enjoy life, and have it in abundance [to the full, till it overflows]."
(John 10:10, AMP)
Your Daily Notes-

"It is an honor for a man to cease from strife..." (Proverbs 20:3, KJV)

Your Daily Notes-

"So let's not get tired of doing what is good. At just the right time we will reap a harvest of blessing if we don't give up." (Galatians 6:9, NLT)

Your Daily Notes-

"Cast all your anxiety on him because he cares for you." (1 Peter 5:7, NIV)

Your Daily Notes-

"Blessed [joyful, nourished by God's goodness] are those who hunger and thirst for righteousness [those who actively seek right standing with God], for they will be [completely] satisfied."
(Matthew 5:6, AMP)

Your Daily Notes-

"Let your light shine before others, so that they may see your good works and give glorify to your Father who is in heaven." (Matthew 5:16, ESV)

Your Daily Notes-

"I will instruct you and teach you in the way which you should go; I will counsel you with my eye upon you." (Psalm 32:8, ESV)

Your Daily Notes-

He gives [blessings] to His beloved even in his sleep" (Psalm 127:2, AMP)

Your Daily Notes-

"If you have faith as small as a mustard seed, you can say to this mulberry tree, 'Be uprooted and planted in the sea,' and it will obey you." (Luke 17:6, NIV)

Your Daily Notes-

"This Book of the Law shall not depart from your mouth, but you shall read [and meditate on] it day and night, so that you may be careful to do [everything] in accordance with all that is written in it; for then you will make your way prosperous, and then you will be successful." (Joshua 1:8, AMP)

Your Daily Notes-

"When you draw close to God, God will draw close to you..." (James 4:8, TLB)

Your Daily Notes-

"He changes times and seasons..." (Daniel 2:21, NIV)

Your Daily Notes-

"Blessed are the meek, for they shall inherit the earth." (Matthew 5:5, NKJV)

Your Daily Notes-

“Great peace have those who love your law, and nothing shall make them stumble.” (Psalm 119:165, NIV)

Your Daily Notes-

“Many are the afflictions of the righteous, but the LORD delivers him out of them all.” (Psalm 34:19, NKJV)

Your Daily Notes-

"The eyes of the Lord run to and fro throughout the whole earth, to show Himself strong on behalf of those whose heart is loyal to Him..." (2 Chronicles 16:9, NKJV)

Your Daily Notes-

"And my God will supply all your needs according to His riches in glory in Christ Jesus." (Philippians 4:19, NASB)

Your Daily Notes-

"Surely goodness and mercy shall follow me all the days of my life; and I will dwell in the house of the Lord forever." (Psalm 23:6, NKJV)

Your Daily Notes-

"No eye has seen, no ear has heard, no mind has conceived what God has prepared for those who love him." (1 Corinthians 2:9, NIV)

Your Daily Notes-

“May the Lord, the God of your fathers, increase you a thousand times and bless you as he has promised!” (Deuteronomy 1:11, NIV)

Your Daily Notes-

“He gives strength to the weary and increases the power of the weak.” (Isaiah 40:29, NIV)

Your Daily Notes-

"I will say of the Lord, He is my Refuge and my Fortress, my God; on Him I lean and rely, and in Him I [confidently] trust." (Psalm 91:2, AMP)

Your Daily Notes-

"Your kingdom come, your will be done, on earth as it is in heaven." (Matthew 6:10, NIV)

Your Daily Notes-

"Then He arose and rebuked the wind, and said to the sea, 'Peace, be still!' And the wind ceased and there was a great calm." (Mark 4:39, NKJV)

Your Daily Notes-

"Where there is no vision...the people perish..." (Proverbs 29:18, AMP)

Your Daily Notes-

"In the morning, Lord, you hear my voice; in the morning I lay my requests before you and wait expectantly." (Psalm 5:3, NIV)

Your Daily Notes-

___

___

___

___

___

"But those who wait for the Lord [who expect, look for, and hope in Him] shall change and renew their strength and power; they shall lift their wings and mount up [close to God] as eagles [mount to up to the sun]; they shall run and not be weary, they shall walk and not faint or become tired."
(Isaiah 40:31, AMP)

Your Daily Notes-

___

___

___

___

___

“Don’t be misled—you cannot mock the justice of God. You will always harvest what you plant.”
(Galatians 6:7, NLT)
Your Daily Notes-

“Instead of your shame you will receive a double portion, and instead of disgrace you will rejoice in your inheritance. And so you will inherit a double portion in your land, and everlasting joy will be yours.”
(Isaiah 61:7, NIV)

Your Daily Notes-

“Dear friends, do not be surprised at the fiery ordeal that has come on you to test you, as though something strange were happening to you. But rejoice inasmuch as you participate in the sufferings of Christ, so that you may be overjoyed when his glory is revealed.” (1 Peter 4:12–13, NIV)

Your Daily Notes-

“I have given you authority...to overcome all the power of the enemy; nothing will harm you.”
(Luke 10:19, NIV)

Your Daily Notes-

"This is my command—be strong and courageous! Do not be afraid or discouraged. For the LORD your God is with you wherever you go."
(Joshua 1:9, NLT)

Your Daily Notes-

"For God is the one who provides seed for the farmer and then bread to eat In the same way, he will provide and increase your resources and then produce a great harvest of generosity in you."
(2 Corinthians 9:10, NLT)

Your Daily Notes-

"Call on Me in the day of trouble; I will deliver you, and you shall honor and glorify Me."
(Psalm 50:15, AMPC)

Your Daily Notes-

"That person is like a tree planted by streams of water, which yields its fruit in season and whose leaf does not wither—whatever they do prospers." (Psalm 1:3, NIV)

Your Daily Notes-

“I have fought a good fight, I have finished my course, I have kept the faith." (2 Timothy 4:7, KJV)

Your Daily Notes-

"You will go out in joy and be led forth in peace…" (Isaiah 55:12, NIV)

Your Daily Notes-

"The thief comes only to steal and kill and destroy; I have come that they may have life, and have it to the full." (John 10:10, NIV)

Your Daily Notes-

"For whoever finds me finds life, and obtains favor from the LORD." (Proverbs 8:35, NKJV)

Your Daily Notes-

"He will be like a tree firmly planted by streams of water, which yields its fruit in its season and its leaf does not wither; and in whatever he does, he prospers." (Psalm 1:3, NASB)

Your Daily Notes-

"Arise, shine; for your light has come! And the glory of the LORD is risen upon you."
(Isaiah 60:1, NKJV)

Your Daily Notes-

"Be strong and courageous. Do not be frightened, and do not be dismayed, for the LORD your God is with you wherever you go." (Joshua 1:9, ESV)

Your Daily Notes-

"The one who guards a fig tree will eat its fruit…" (Proverbs 27:18, NIV)

Your Daily Notes-

"For I know the thoughts and plans I have for you…to give you hope in your final outcome."
(Jeremiah 29:11, AMPC)

Your Daily Notes-

"Though the fig tree may not blossom, nor fruit be on the vines…yet I will rejoice in the Lord, I will joy in the God of my salvation."
(Habakkuk 3:17-18, NKJV)

Your Daily Notes-

"…I focus on this one thing: Forgetting the past and looking forward to what lies ahead"
(Philippians 3:13, NLT)

Your Daily Notes-

"Now He who supplies seed to the sower and bread for food will supply and multiply your seed for sowing and increase the harvest of your righteousness." (2 Corinthians 9:10, NASB)

Your Daily Notes-

"...the appetite of the diligent is abundantly supplied." (Proverbs 13:4, AMPC)

Your Daily Notes-

"About midnight Paul and Silas were praying and singing hymns to God, and the other prisoners were listening to them. Suddenly there was such a violent earthquake that the foundations of the prison were shaken. At once all the prison doors flew open, and everyone's chains came loose."
(Acts 16:25-26, NIV)
Your Daily Notes-

"...And in an instant, suddenly, you shall be visited and delivered by the Lord of hosts..."
(Isaiah 29:5-6, AMPC)

Your Daily Notes-

"You will keep him in perfect peace, whose mind is stayed on You, because he trusts in You."
(Isaiah 26:3, NKJV)

Your Daily Notes-

"‘Don't be afraid,’ the prophet answered. ‘Those who are with us are more than those who are with them.’" (2 Kings 6:16, NIV)

Your Daily Notes-

“May God Bless you, to get you through those battles, which no one will ever see”

Thank You

Printed in Great Britain
by Amazon